THE
JANUARY
BABY

By Noel Streatfeild and available from Headline

The January Baby

The February Baby

The March Baby

The April Baby

The May Baby

The June Baby

The July Baby

The August Baby

The September Baby

The October Baby

The November Baby

The December Baby

THE
January
BABY

★

Noel Streatfeild

First published in 1959
This edition published in 2023 by Headline Home
an imprint of Headline Publishing Group

I

Cataloguing in Publication Data is available from the British Library

Hardback ISBN 978 1 0354 0839 9
eISBN 978 1 0354 0840 5

Typeset in 14.75/15pt Centaur MT Pro by Jouve (UK), Milton Keynes

Printed and bound in Great Britain by Clays Ltd, Elcograf S.p.A.

HEADLINE PUBLISHING GROUP
An Hachette UK Company
Carmelite House
50 Victoria Embankment
London EC4Y 0DZ

www.headline.co.uk
www.hachette.co.uk

CONTENTS

A BABY has been born. The great news has flown from mouth to mouth. How is the mother? Is it a boy or a girl? How much does the baby weigh? Has the baby any hair? Who does the baby look like? Then at last comes the news that mother and baby are receiving visitors. At once the problem arises, what present shall I take?

From the moment the news of the baby was known, flowers have been arriving. It is never possible in our own homes to have too many flowers, but if the baby has been born in a nursing home or hospital, especially if the mother has not a private room, it is more than possible to have too many flowers. A probationer nurse, otherwise gaiety itself, can look shattered when the sixtieth bunch arrives, and say with resignation 'I am afraid it will have to be a jam-pot this time.'

Flower presents in January are likely, unless they come from the most fabulously expensive shop, to look rather alike. Mimosa and carnations perhaps from the south of France. Narcissus and daffodils from the Scilly Isles. Anemones from Cornwall. Or there might be a cyclamen or hyacinth in a pot – a lovely present except for the heart searchings when the mother leaves: ought a pot plant to be left behind, or can it with decency be taken home?

3

Fruit is a nice present, but the baby doesn't eat fruit, and mother can only get through so much, and if she wants fruit she has generally asked her nearest and dearest to provide it. So unless it is possible to get hold of exotics, such as lychees, perhaps which it is known that the mother adores, fruit is out. Different in the summer when somebody else will enjoy the cherries, strawberries, wall peaches, or raspberries the mother does not want, but it is not easy to get rid of surplus oranges, bananas, and apples.

Something to wear is perfect, but mostly the something to wear was sent before the

baby arrived. Frocks, matinee jackets, shawls, in fact an entire wardrobe has been streaming in for months. Most of the clothes, it is true, will not fit until the baby is six months old at least. But for the new baby nothing is wanted, for everything has of course been made or obtained by the mother.

The mothers of January babies suffer because January is so soon after Christmas.

When Christmas presents were being thought out, and a present for the mother-to-be was chosen, thoughts flew naturally to bed jackets and night-dresses. A pity now, thinks the visitor, how nice to have turned up with a pretty warm bed jacket, but I have already sent her one.

It is years of wondering what present shall I bring, that has resulted in this book. The contents were selected by experience. It would seem to the visitor as if the days after the baby is born would be carefree with nothing to do from one end of the day to the other. Nothing apparently is further from the truth. 'I don't get time to get down to a book,' says the mother, 'something is always happening, if it isn't baby's feeds, it's my meals, or my bed is being made, or I'm doing exercises. I never get time to settle down to anything for long.' All right, short reading then, nothing of great length.

Names came next to mind. The first question everybody asks is 'What are you going to call your baby?' It turns up regularly like 'What are you going to be when you grow up?' It is a tiresome question, because obviously if the parents know what they are calling their child, they have already announced it, either in a paper or by word of mouth. But there are many who simply cannot make up their minds. Having agreed on a family name, or to call him after the man who is to be his godfather, or her after mother's best friend, there are still second, and even third names to be thought of. The

chosen name may sound awful with the surname, and there are initials to worry about — is it kind to land the child with W.C. as a trademark for life? Here then, for you, mother, are a selection of possibles, almost all connected with January.

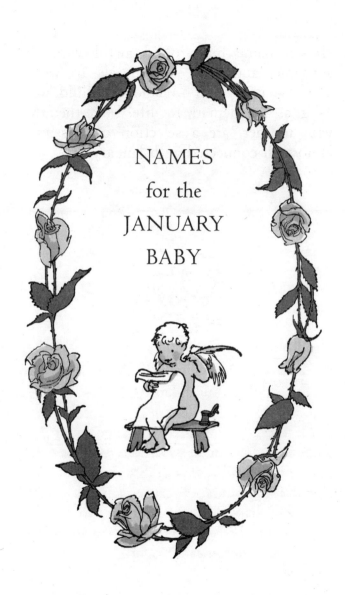

NAMES
for the
JANUARY
BABY

*J*AN, *Janet, Janice, Janine* and *Janis* are all connected with January.

Jane and *John* mean 'The Lord's Grace.' *Jan* for a boy makes a change from *John*. *Evan, Hans, Iain* or *Ian, Ivan, Jack, Sean* or *Shawn* and *Shane* are all forms of *John*.

Bertha is suitable because it is associated with Epiphany which is on the 6th January. *Clara, Elaine, Eleanor, Ellen, Helen, Lena* and *Phoebe*, as well as *Bertha*, mean 'bright.'

The first Monday after Twelfth Night is called Plough Monday, this is because it was the first day after Christmas when husbandmen went back to their ploughing. If you like a name suitable for a tiller of the soil *George*, *Geordie* and *Yorrick* mean 'tiller of the soil' and *Bartholomew* and *Bartley* mean 'abounding in furrows'.

On the 8th January is St Lucian's Day. *Lucian* means 'the light'. From *Lucian* comes the boy's name *Lucius* and the girls' names *Lucia*, *Lucilla*, *Lucinda*, *Lucy* and *Selina*.

The 13th January is St Hilary's Day. *Hilary* means 'cheerful' and is a convenient name because it will do as well for a boy as for a girl.

The 18th January is St Prisca's Day. *Prisca* means 'ancient', not perhaps a very suitable name for a baby, but from it comes *Priscilla* and *Prisca* itself is original and would make a nice Christian name.

On the 20th January St Fabian has his day. *Fabian* means 'bean grower'.

On the 21st January is St Agnes's Day. *Agnes* means 'pure'.

On the 22nd January is St Vincent's Day. *Vincent* means 'conquering'.

On the 24th January is St Timothy's Day. *Timothy* means 'Honour God'.

The Conversion of St Paul is celebrated on the 25th January. *Paul* means 'little'. From *Paul* come the names *Paula*, *Paulette*, *Paulina* and *Pauline*.

The birthstone for January is the Garnet. *Garnet* is another name which could be used either for a boy or a girl.

The Guardian Angel who looks after January children is Gabriel. *Gabriel* means 'strong man of God'. There is a girl's version of *Gabriel* spelt *Gabrielle.*

The Anglo-Saxons found starving wolves such an aggravation during the cold weather they called January 'Wolf Month'. But wolves must have been admired as well as feared for any number of names have something to do with wolves, but in a pleasant way. *Ralph* means 'counsel wolf', *Randall* and *Randolph* 'shield wolf', *Rolfe* and *Rollo* 'wolf fame', and although few mothers and fathers are likely to choose the name today, *Adolph* means 'noble wolf'. Boys were also called after bears: *Arthur* means 'a bear', *Bernard* 'brave as a bear', *Colborn* 'a black bear' and *Thorburn* 'Thor's bear'.

In January we expect snow so a white name is very suitable. All these names mean 'white'.

For the boy *Alban* and for the girl *Blanche,
Candida, Gwenda* and *Winne.*

Boys' names connected with January seem
rather scarce so how about the names of the
famous who are connected with ice and
snow? *Edmund* after Sir Edmund Hillary.
Edmund means 'rich protection'. *Robert*
after Captain Scott. *Robert* means 'bright
fame'. *Laurence* after Captain Oates. *Laurence*
means 'laurel'. *Ernest* after Sir Ernest
Shackleton. *Ernest* means 'vigour'. Or *Martin*

15

after Martin Frobisher. *Martin* is of course a variant of Mars. Flower names to fit the month are charming but there are not of

course many flowers in January, but there is the very early quite delightful witch hazel, so how about *Hazel* for a girl? And *Aileen or Eileen* mean 'hazel' too. Or what about *Ivy*, always with us. Another evergreen to be found in January is the laurel, from which come *Laura*, *Lauren*, and *Loretta*. One of the loveliest of the winter flowers is the winter jasmine which is at its best in January. *Jasmine* is a delicious name for any baby. All gardeners thank the brave little iris stylosa which arrives

miraculously frail and unscarred even in the coldest weather, so how about *Iris*. Of course there are mothers who like names that will be unique to their baby. If that's how you feel I would suggest *Snowdrop*, *Scilla*, or *Camellia*. Or of course, if you wish to be exotic how about

Mimosa, which from Christmas brightens the grey streets with its flaming yellow? *Hyacinth* is not an original name but it is very suitable for January, for how many homes throughout the month smell delicious because of a hyacinth in a pot? Finally, and this I think is a name which would suit a boy just as well as a girl, though I have never heard it used, how about *Frost?*

GIFTS
for the
JANUARY
BABY

IF the godparent or other well-wisher would like to give the baby a piece of jewellery, the right stone for January is the garnet. Mothers of girl babies will probably sigh and wish the January stone was of more value. But the garnet has good qualities about it. It is the emblem of constancy. And here is what Leonardus wrote about it in *The Mirror of Stones*, 1750: 'Its Virtue is to chear the Heart and drive away Sorrow. Some say, it defends the Bearer of it from pestilential Diseases.'

The very pretty custom of knowing the meaning of flowers and so arranging a bouquet or vase that it sent a message has long been neglected. Yet in every month of the year flowers can be found growing wild that, properly arranged, convey words to the recipient. If your baby should receive a bowl of snowdrops arranged in moss, here is what the present means.

'Hope' is the emblematic meaning of the snowdrop and moss stands for 'Maternal Love'.

If your baby was born between the 1st and the 20th January read pages 26 and 27, but if between the 21st and the 31st skip to pages 28 and 29.

UNDER
WHAT STARS WAS
MY BABY
BORN?

CAPRICORN
The Sea Goat

22nd Dec–20th January

AQUARIUS
The Water Bearer

21st January–18th February

PISCES
The Fishes

19th February–20th March

ARIES
The Ram

21st March–20th April

TAURUS
The Bull

21st April–21st May

GEMINI
The Twins

22nd May–21st June

CANCER
The Crab

22nd June–23rd July

LEO
The Lion

24th July–23rd August

VIRGO
The Virgin

24th Aug–23rd Sept

LIBRA
The Scales

24th Sept–23rd Oct

SCORPIO
The Scorpion

24th Oct–22nd Nov

SAGITTARIUS
The Archer

23rd Nov–21st Dec

Capricorn — the Sea Goat
22nd December—20th January

PEOPLE born under Capricorn are deep thinkers, ambitious for intellectual attainments and political power. They are good organizers and often splendid orators, speaking rapidly and urgently. They are self-reliant and proud, yet very persistent and patient. Their magnetism and self-possession make them good teachers. Capricorn people are faithful and sincere in their affections, but they are not demonstrative. Their crust of apparent self-ishness covers little vanity, but a real earnestness. They are more capable of carrying out large undertakings than people of any other sign.

For the Capricorn Baby

Lucky to wear a sapphire.
Lucky stones are jet, onyx and lapis lazuli.
Lucky metal is lead.
The Capricorn baby's colour is indigo.
Lucky number is 8.
Luckiest day of the week is Saturday.

Aquarius — the Waterbearer
21st January—18th February

PEOPLE born under Aquarius are either very strong or very weak, for their power is spiritual, and it remains for them to discover and harness it. They are nervous and thin skinned, often possessing a high degree of artistic sensibility. They are good looking and gentle of voice. As friends they are true, though seemingly detached. Aquarius people have a special gift for character reading, and their invariable kind heartedness may put this extraordinary knowledge of human nature to work towards humanitarian ends.

For the Aquarius baby

Lucky to wear a sapphire, a lynx-eye onyx.
Lucky stones are jet, lapis lazuli, black
    basalt.
Lucky metal is lead.
The Aquarius baby's colour is indigo.
Lucky number is 8.
Luckiest day of the week is Saturday.

BABIES BORN
ON
THE SAME DAY
AS
YOUR BABY

IS there any virtue in being born on a particular day? Is there any truth that babies born under Capricorn are like this and under Aquarius like that? Read the following list and decide for yourself.

1st   Lorenzo 'the Magnificent' de' Medici, 1450. Maria Edgeworth, 1767. Edward Stanley, Bishop of Norwich, 1779. Francis Egerton, 1st Earl of Ellesmere, 1800. E. M. Forester, 1879. Dana Andrews, 1912. Raymond Pellegrin, 1925.

2nd   General James Wolfe, 1727. Gilbert Murray, 1866. Count Folke Bernadotte, 1895. Anthony Armstrong, 1897. Vera Zorina, 1917. Duke of Devonshire, 1920.

3rd   Cicero, 106 B.C. Sir Henry Lytton, 1867. Earl Attlee, 1883. Herbert

S. Morrison, 1888. Sir John Slessor,
1897. Ray Milland, 1908. Bill
Travers, 1922.

4th   Jacob Grimm, 1785. Sir Isaac Pitman,
1813. Augustus John, 1879. Jane Wyman,
1914.

5th   Adenauer, 1876.

6th   Richard, King of the Romans,
1209. Richard II, 1367. Gustave
Doré, 1833. Stella Benson, 1892. Sir
Edwin Plowden, 1907. Loretta Young,
1914.

7th   Thomas of Woodstock, 1355. Saint
Pius V, 1504. Princess Charlotte of
Wales, 1796. Bernadette of Lourdes,
1844.

8th   Wilkie Collins, 1824. Baron von
Bülow, 1830. Earl of Rosebery, 1882.
Bronsilava Nijinska, 1891. Mary
Elizabeth Jenkin, 1892. S. Bandaraneike,
1899. Malenkov, 1902. Jose Ferrer,
1912.

9th   Gracie Fields, 1898. Richard Nixon,
1913 (Vice-President of the USA).

10th   Margaret of Austria, 1480. Marshal
Ney, 1769.

11th   William James, 1842. George Nathaniel Curzon, 1st Marquess, 1859. Eva Le Gallienne, 1899. Pierre Mendès-France, 1907. Anthony Nutting, 1920. Neville Duke, 1922.

12th   Charles Perrault, 1628. Edmund Burke, 1729. George Villiers, 4th Earl of Clarendon, 1800. Paul Taglioni, 1808. Marshal Joffre, 1852. Jack London, 1876. Louis Renault, 1877. Kurt Joos, 1901. Luise Rainer, 1912.

13th   Patrick Hume, 1st Earl of Marchmont, 1641. Sir W. Reid Dick, 1879.

14th   Pierre Loti, 1850. Albert Schweitzer, 1875. Pastor Martin Niëmoller, 1892.

Cecil Beaton, 1904. Robert Speaight, 1904.

15th   Philip 'the Bold,' Duke of Burgundy, 1342. Jean Coralli, 1779. Ivor Novello, 1893. Dr Charles Hill, 1904. Gamal Abdel Nasser, 1918.

16th   Edmund 'Crouchback,' Earl of Lancaster and Derby, 1245. Edward Gordon Craig, 1872. Diana Wynyard, 1906.

17th   Benjamin Franklin, 1706. Mrs Henry Wood, 1814. Anne Brontë, 1820. Catherine Booth, 1829. Chekhov, 1860. David Lloyd George, 1863. Sir Compton MacKenzie, 1883. Sir Walter Monckton, 1891. Nevil Shute, 1899. Moira Shearer, 1926.

18th   Austin Dobson, 1840. A. A. Milne, 1882. Oliver Hardy, 1892. Cary Grant, 1904. Danny Kaye, 1913.

19th   James Watt, 1736. Edgar Allan Poe, 1809. Paul Cézanne, 1839.

20th   Elizabeth of Bohemia, 1292. Charles III of Spain, 1716.

21st   General Weygand, 1867. Commander

Sir Stephen King-Hall, 1893. Christian Dior, 1905. Paul Scofield, 1922.

22nd   Francis Bacon, 1561. André Ampère, 1775. Lord Byron, 1788. Strindberg, 1849. Beatrice Potter Webb, 1858. D. W. Griffith, 1875. Constance Collier, 1878. Charles Morgan, 1894.

23rd   Adelina de Lara, 1872. Princess Caroline of Monaco, 1957. Stendhal, 1783.

24th   Hadrian, A.D. 76. Frederick the Great, 1712. Hoffman, 1776. Vicki Baum, 1896. Duncan Sandys, 1908. Ann Todd, 1909.

25th   Robert Burns, 1759. W. Somerset Maugham, 1874. Frances Pitt, J.P., 1888.

26th   Lord George Sackville, 1716. Jean Baptiste Bernadotte, later Charles XIV of Sweden, 1763. Oscar Asche, 1871. General Douglas MacArthur, 1880. Henry Cotton, 1907. Jill Esmond, 1908.

27th   Mozart, 1756. Lewis Carroll, 1832. Jerome Kern, 1885.

28th   Henry VII, 1457. Pope Clement IX, 1600. Artur Rubinstein, 1886. Colette, 1873.

29th   Frederick Delius, 1862. Romain

Rolland, 1866. Sir William Rothenstein, 1872.

30th   Angela Thirkell, 1890. Thornton Wilder, 1902. John Profumo, 1915.

31st   Anna Pavlova, 1885. Mario Lanza, 1921. Jean Simmons, 1929. Princess Beatrix of the Netherlands, 1938.

38

THE
UPBRINGING
OF JANUARY
BABIES
OF
THE
PAST

J UST as it can be pleasant to look at the
frost and the sleet from the window of a
well-warmed room, so it can increase
your satisfaction that all is well with your
baby when you compare upbringing plans for
it with the upbringing endured by unfortunate
babies of the past.

'It was the practice of all Celtic nations to
plunge their new-born infants into some lake
or river, even in the winter season, with a view
to try the firmness of their constitution and to
harden their bodies.'

*The Englishwoman's Domestic
Magazine,* 1860.

A GOOD STOMACH PLASTER FOR A BEWITCHED CHILD

Take a little of the oil of almonds, a little deer's tallow, as much of rose vinegar and one ounce of caraway seed. All these articles pounded together, put upon a blue paper, and lay it upon the child's stomach.

But before using the plaster, the mother must, after eating supper, cut three pieces of bread thin, while sticking the knife three times through the bread, and put this knife under the child's bed during the night. If the child is bewitched, the knife will be rusty all over on the next morning; then take the bread from the knife, put butter thereon, and give it to a black dog to eat, while you must put an old shirt on the child, which, after remaining for three days and three nights upon the child's person, must be taken off and interred with the above mentioned plaster. This has to be done noiselessly, before sunrise, and under an elderwood shrub.

Albertus Magnus, *White and Black Art for Man and Beast* 13th C., trans. *c.* 1880.

The present management of children in Spain is very curious – how the babies live is a matter for wonder. They now wear the same kind of swaddling clothes that were fashionable in the time of Herod. The baby is placed at the end of a long piece of coarse flannel, the colour of mustard – all the Spanish flannel appears to be of this intense yellow colour, and as thick as a blanket and rolled up to the top – leaving nothing but its head out; then it is pinned up tightly, and looks like a little mummy. Thus enveloped, the babies are of course perfectly stiff, so that they can be raised up on end in a corner, but how the mothers carry them it is not easy to imagine.

Bits about Babies, 1870.

REMEDY FOR WHOOPING-COUGH

. . . to ask the rider of a piebald horse, 'What's good for the chin-cough?' and to follow his directions.

One day in the winter of 1878–9, a near relative of my own was driving a pair of ponies, one a grey roan, and the other a white one, very slightly 'flea-bitten,' when as he drew up at Newport railway-station, up rushed an excited woman, crying out, 'Eh, mester, what's good for the chin-cough?' 'Oh, you've come to the wrong man,' said he. 'Eh, wunna it do? I thought this 'ud do as well!' and she went away much disappointed.

Jackson, Shropshire Folk-Lore, 1883.

Our history is pock-marked with little entries like the following:

'On and after the first day of January, 1893, no child under the age of eleven years shall be employed in a factory or workshop.'

Factory Acts.

And here is a pathetic description of what sometimes happened to small boys. It comes from the *Memoirs of The Lady Hester Stanhope as related by herself in conversations with her physician,* 1845.

'MOUNT LEBANON. — Servants work twice as hard in England as they do here. Why, there was the boy of twelve or thirteen years old that used to go to Sevenoaks to fetch papa's letters. Every day but one in the week did that boy ride backward and forward; and sometimes I have seen him lifted off his horse,

with his fingers so benumbed that he could not even ring the bell; and his face and hands were rubbed with snow, and he was walked about for a quarter of an hour before he was allowed to go into the servants' hall.'

And here is an illuminating advertisement published in *The Times* in 1809. Even with every kindness swapping a son for a daughter seems a bit harsh.

'TO MASTERS OF ACADEMIES. — A Lady who keeps a Boarding School of respectability, a few miles from Town, in a delightful situation, wishes to meet with a Gentleman who would place a Daughter or Niece under her care, in exchange for her Son, who is about 8 years of age. The strictest care and attention should be paid to her health, morals, and improvement, and the same kindness shown she would wish her own child to receive. Address, post paid, for A.B. at Mr Stratton's, No. 47, Piccadilly. An Apprentice wanted in the same School.'

A
*ROYAL JANUARY
BABY*

THE Princess Royal, Duchess of Würtemberg, writes to Lady Elgin, governess of Princess Charlotte of Wales, who was born on 7th January, 1796.

'Louisberg: October 2, 1801.

Am I to say everything I think? I regret much the weakness of the mother in making a plaything of the child, and not reflecting that she is a Princess and not an actress. Were she my daughter, I should try and teach her everything I know, but never let her show the little knowledge unless to her nearest relations, and persuade her that she can be of no consequence to anybody else unless as she grows up she makes herself beloved by her good qualities. I am not fond of children learning by heart, because it too frequently leads their parents to make a show of them, which by degrees takes away that modesty and diffidence which are so charming in youth. As she has once found out she is clever, nothing but being with older children will ever get the better of this unfortunate vanity, which is a little in her blood, as you full well know. I approve very much of your trying to get the better of her covetousness. As she has been inoculated, when you are in the country you should lead her into some cottage where the children are all in rags and in want of food, and see whether such scenes of distress would not soften her heart, particularly if you would have some clothes made in the house, and some days afterwards show her those very objects clean and happy. I am a great enemy to giving to beggars, and believe as much care must be taken to teach young people to give properly as to be charitable.'

As a result perhaps of that visit to the cottage where all the children were in rags is the following page from the Princess

Charlotte's account book which shows the child did not accept the Princess Royal's views on giving alms to beggars. Surely few children at the age of six have given so large a proportion of their income to charity and, indeed, few have kept such clear accounts.

1802

February	s.	d.
In hand	11	1
Received for playing a new lesson	1	0
Received	5	0
Received	6	5
Received	10	6
	£1 14	0

1802

February	s.	d.
20 A poor Frenchman	2	6
To a chalk pencil	0	2
25 A poor man	1	0
March		
1 A poor woman	1	0
5 Poor man	1	6

7	A lame man	1	0
13	To seeing a house	2	0
	A poor man	1	0
	To two men last week	2	0
22	To 3 different poor	2	6
30	To poor	3	6
	To do. paid by Mr Lyons	3	4

April

	To the old woman with the ass	2	6
6	An old soldier	1	0
	The old sailor twice	2	0
	A man and a boy with a hand organ	4	0
	The poor this week	3	0
		£1 14	0

A Brief Memoir of the Princess Charlotte of Wales,
by the Lady Rose Weigall, 1874.

DISTINGUISHED
JANUARY
BABIES

THE HON. ROBERT BOYLE
born January, 1627.

H E was nursed by an Irish nurse, after the Irish manner, wher they putt the child into a pendulous satchell instead of a cradle, with a slitt for the child's head to peepe out.

Aubrey, *Lives of Eminent Men*, 1813.

MARJORIE FLEMING
born January, 1803.

Oh! Isa, pain did visit me,
    I was at the last extremity;
How often did I think of you,
    I wished your graceful form to view
To clasp you in my weak embrace
    Indeed I thought I'd run my race:
Good care, I'm sure, was of me taken,
    But still indeed, I was much shaken,
At last I daily strength did gain,
    And oh! at last away went pain;
At length the doctor thought I might
    Stay in the parlor all the night;
I now continue so to do
    Farewell to Nancy and to you.
                        Written by herself, 1811.

JAMES WATT
born January, 1736.

When not quite fourteen his parents planned for him to stay for a while with a family friend in Glasgow, but Mrs Campbell soon wrote asking to be relieved of her guest: 'I cannot stand the excitement he keeps me in. I am worn out for want of sleep. Every evening, before retiring to rest, he contrives to engage me in conversation, then begins some striking tale, and whether humorous or pathetic, the interest is so overpowering, that the family all listen to him with breathless attention, and hour after hour strikes unheeded.'

Smiles, *Lives of Boulton and Watt*, 1865.

born January, 1756.

When he was four years old, Court Trumpeter Schachtner, visiting his house one day, found him at work writing a piano concerto. 'His father took it from him and showed me the notes written on an inky surface. (Wolfgang dipped his pen right down into the inkstand, as all children do, so that after each dip when the pen touched the paper, blots fell. The remedy he had found was to smear the ink with the palm of his hand and then write his notes over the smears.)'

Nohl, *Mozart*, 1863.

BENJAMIN FRANKLIN
born January, 1706.

When embarked with other children, the helm was commonly deputed to me, particularly on difficult occasions; and, in every other project, I was almost always the leader of the troop, whom I sometimes involved in embarrassments. I shall give an instance of this, which demonstrates an early disposition of mind for public enterprises, though the one in question was not conducted by justice.

The mill-pond was terminated on one side by a marsh, upon the borders of which we were accustomed to take our stand, at high water, to angle for small fish. By dint of walking, we had converted the place into a perfect quagmire. My proposal was to erect a wharf that should afford us firm footing; and I pointed out to my companions a large heap of stones, intended for the building of a new house near the marsh, and which were well adapted for our purpose. Accordingly, when the workmen retired in the evening, I assembled a number of my play-fellows, and by labouring diligently, like ants, sometimes four of us uniting our strength to carry a single stone, we removed them all, and constructed our little quay. The workmen were surprised the next morning at not finding their stones; which had been conveyed to our wharf. Enquiries were made respecting the authors of this conveyance; we were discovered; complaints were exhibited against us; and many of us underwent correction on the part of our parents; and though I strenuously defended the utility of the work, my father at length convinced me, that nothing which was not strictly honest could be useful.

Written by himself, describing his life when aged 11.

MRS ELIZA FLETCHER
born January, 1770.

Reflecting on my experience of a boarding-school as then conducted, I cannot but wonder how any one could escape the peril of such association as might have been met with there. The Manor School was in the hands of a very well-disposed, conscientious old gentlewoman, but of so limited an understanding that, under her rule, mischief of every kind (short of actual vice) was going on without her even suspecting it. Lessons were said by rote, without being understood; servants were bribed to bring in dainties clandestinely; in short, every kind of dissimulation was practised to indemnify the subjects of this petty despotism, for the restraints unnecessarily imposed upon them. During the four years I was at this school, two chapters of the Bible were read every morning by two of the young ladies as a reading lesson. Prayers were regularly drawled out by the husband of our governess, a choleric old man, who thumped our fingers so often for bad writing, with his mahogany ferule, that we listened to his prayers with any feelings but those of love or devotion. I do not remember to have received a single religious impression at this school, though creeds were repeated, and catechisms taught, and all the formalities of religious service regularly performed. Four volumes of the *Spectator* constituted our whole school library. But besides the negative evils of such school life, was the misfortune of having as daily associates some girls of thoroughly depraved character. Two of these, the most remarkable for dissimulation and all evil characteristics, who afterwards married, eloped from their husbands.

This was taken from the autobiography of Mrs Fletcher, describing her school life when she was 11.

LORD BYRON
born January, 1788.

. . . we were both the merest children. I had
and have been attached fifty times since that
period; yet I recollect all we said to each
other, all our caresses, her features, my
restlessness, sleeplessness, my tormenting my
mother's maid to write for me to her, which
she at last did, to quiet me. Poor Nancy
thought I was wild, and, as I could not write
for myself, became my secretary. I remember,
too, our walks, and the happiness of sitting by
Mary, in the children's apartment, at their
house not far from the Plainstones at
Aberdeen, while her lesser sister Helen played

with the doll, and we sat gravely making love, in our way . . .

I wonder if she can have the least remembrance of it or me? or remember her pitying sister Helen for not having an admirer too? How very pretty is the perfect image of her in my memory – her brown, dark hair, and hazel eyes; her very dress! I should be quite grieved to see *her now*; the reality, however beautiful, would destroy, or at least confuse, the features of the lovely Peri which then existed in her, and still lives in my imagination, at the distance of more than sixteen years.

Letters and Journals of Lord Byron, 1830, describing a love affair when he was eight.

GAMES
for the
JANUARY
BABY

A FACE-GAME

THE nurse says:
'Knock at the door, (tapping the child's forehead).
Ring at the bell, (pulling an ear).
Peep through the keyhole, (encircling an eye with her finger and thumb).
Lift up the latch, (pulling the nose).
Wipe your shoes, (stroking the upper lip).
Walk in, (putting her finger in the mouth).
Chin, chin, chin, chocker! (chucking under the chin).'

Jackson, *Shropshire Folk-Lore*, 1883.

GEE-GEE

The baby sits on mother's foot. The foot
moves in time to the rhyme. The child holds
mother's hands as if they were reins.

A gee-gee and a gentleman
     Went out to ride one day.
Saying Horsey-Porsey. Walky-Walky. Trotty,
     oh so gay.
     But the horse to jumping took,
And the man with terror shook,
     And they neither looked so happy at the
          end of the day.
Saying Horsey-Porsey. Jumpy-Pumpy Trotty-
          Watty – Walking all the way.

GAME OF THE FOX

One child is Fox. He has a knotted handkerchief, and a home to which he may go whenever he is tired, but while out of home he must always hop on one leg. The other children are geese, and have no home. When the Fox is coming out he says:

> The Fox gives warning
> It's a cold frosty morning.

After he has said these words he is at liberty to hop out, and use his knotted handkerchief. Whoever he can touch is Fox instead, but the geese run on two legs, and if the Fox puts his other leg down, he is hunted back to his home.

Halliwell, *Popular Rhymes and Nursery Tales*,
1849.

A JANUARY
CHILD IN
FICTION

I, being the younger by five or six years, was always regarded as the *child*, and the pet of the family: father, mother, and sister all combined to spoil me — not by foolish indulgence to render me fractious and ungovernable, but by ceaseless kindness to make me too helpless and dependent — too unfit for buffeting with the cares and turmoils of life.

Mary and I were brought up in the strictest seclusion. My mother, being at once highly accomplished, well informed, and fond of employment, took the whole charge of our education on herself, with the exception of Latin — which my father undertook to teach us — so that we never even went to school; and, as there was no society in the neighbourhood, our only intercourse with the world consisted in a stately tea-party, now and then, with the principal farmers and tradespeople of the vicinity (just to avoid being stigmatised as too proud to consort with our neighbours), and an annual visit to our paternal grandfather's; where himself, our kind grandmamma, a maiden aunt, and two or three elderly ladies and gentlemen, were the only persons we ever saw. Sometimes our mother would amuse us with stories and anecdotes of her younger days, which, while they entertained us amazingly, frequently awoke – in *me*, at least – a secret wish to see a little more of the world.

Anne Brontë, *Agnes Grey*, 1847.

Lucy was a good little girl, and always minded what was said to her, and was very attentive whenever her father or mother had taught her anything. So her mother taught her to read and to work, and when she was six years old she could employ herself, without being troublesome to anybody. She could work for herself, and for her brother, and sometimes, when Lucy behaved very well, her mother let her do a little work for her, or for her father. Her mother had given her a little thimble, to put upon her finger, and a little housewife, to keep her needles and thread in, and a little pair of scissors, to cut her thread with, and a little work-bag, to put her work in; and Lucy's father had given her a little book, to read in, whenever she pleased, and she could read in it by herself, and understand all she read, and learn everything that was in it.

Maria Edgeworth, *Early Lessons*, 1837.

LETTERS
from
JANUARY
CHILDREN

MY DEAR ISA,
I now sit down to answer all your kind and beloved letters, which you was so good as to write to me. This is the first time I ever wrote a letter in all my life. There are a great many girls in the square, and they cry just like a pig when we are under the painful necessity of putting him to death. Miss Potune, a lady of my acquaintance, praises me dreadfully. I repeated something out of Deen Sweft, and she said I was fit for the stage, and you may think I was primmed up with majestick pride, but upon my word I felt myself turn a little birsay (birsay is a word that William composed, which is, as you may suppose, a little enraged).

This horid fat simpliton says that my aunt is beautifull, which is intirely impossible, for that is not her nature.

MARJORIE FLEMING.

Derby, March 30, 1776.

DEAR MAMMA,

It is with the greatest pleasure I write to you, as I flatter myself it will make you happy to hear from me. I hope you and my dear papa are well. School now seems agreeable to me. I have begun French and dancing, and intend to make great improvement in everything I learn. I know that it will give you great satisfaction to hear that I am a good girl. My cousin Clay sends her love to you; mine to my brothers and sisters, who I hope are well. Pray give my duty to papa, and accept the same from, dear mamma,

YOUR DUTIFUL DAUGHTER.
From Maria Edgeworth, born January, 1767.

HERE IS A LETTER FROM LORD BYRON.

Newstead Abbey, Novr 8th, 1798.

DEAR MADAM,

My Mamma being unable to write herself desires I will let you know that the potatoes are now ready and you are welcome to them whenever you please. She begs you will ask Mrs Parkyns if she would wish the poney to go round by Nottingham or to go home the nearest way as it is now quite well but too small to carry me. I have sent a young Balbit which I beg Miss Frances will accept off and which I promised to send before. My Mamma desires her best compliments to you all in which I join.

I am Dear Aunt
Yours sincerely
BYRON.

I hope you will excuse all blunders as it is the first letter I ever wrote.

RHYMES
for the
JANUARY
BABY

J ANUARY brings the snow,
Makes our feet and fingers glow.
                    Sara Coleridge (1802–1852).

HUMPTY DUMPTY'S SONG

In winter, when the fields are white,
I sing this song for your delight . . .

In spring, when woods are getting green,
I'll try and tell you what I mean.

In summer, when the days are long,
Perhaps you'll understand the song:

In autumn, when the leaves are brown,
Take pen and ink, and write it down.

I sent a message to the fish:
I told them 'This is what I wish.'

The little fishes of the sea
They sent an answer back to me.

The little fishes' answer was
'We cannot do it, Sir, because . . .'

I sent to them again to say,
'It will be better to obey.'

The fishes answered with a grin
'Why, what a temper you are in!'

I told them once, I told them twice:
They would not listen to advice.

I took a kettle large and new,
Fit for the deed I had to do.

My heart went hop, my heart went thump;
I filled the kettle at the pump.

Then some one came to me and said
'The little fishes are in bed.'

I said to him, I said it plain,
'Then you must wake them up again.'

I said it very loud and clear;
I went and shouted in his ear.

But he was very stiff and proud;
He said 'You needn't shout so loud!'

And he was very proud and stiff;
He said 'I'd go and wake them, if . . .'

I took a corkscrew from the shelf:
I went to wake them up myself.

And when I found the door was locked,
I pulled and pushed and kicked and
   knocked.

And when I found the door was shut
I tried to turn the handle, but . . .

Lewis Carroll (1832–1898).

NEW YEAR'S RESOLUTIONS

(To be sung to the air of *Comiti' thro' the Rye*.)

I'll try to do as I am bid;
I'll try to please mamma;
I'll try to learn my lesson too,
And spell to my papa.

When children want my pretty toys,
Or little picture book,
I'll try at once to give them up,
And see how pleased they look.

Kingston, *Infant Amusements*, 1867.

81

A PRAYER

Gentle Jesus, meek and mild,
Look upon a little child.
Pity my simplicity,
And teach me, Lord, to pray to Thee.
Fain I would to Thee be brought,
Dearest Lord, forbid it not.

Short and Simple Prayers, 1844.

GOODNIGHT
to the
JANUARY
BABY

IF twelve fairies could each give your baby one wish, what would you choose? Twelve is a lot: you could have brilliant brains, beauty, a happy disposition, riches, fame, a saintly character, great wisdom, outstanding talent, wit, a sense of humour, generosity, and a great capacity for love. Which would you ask for? Would you choose a little of each? Would you remember the thirteenth fairy with her known ability for throwing a spanner in the works? Perhaps, and I suspect this is what would really happen, you would dismiss the fairies gratefully but firmly, saying 'Thank you my dear fairies, I don't want a wish. You see I have no wish to change my January baby. I love it just the way it is.'

Noel Streatfeild